Be a Wife

Not a Knife

Fight Him with Prayer

by

Shenine Wiggs

Be a Wife, Not a Knife

Copyright © 2017 by Shenine Wiggs

DEDICATION

"Therefore, what God has joined together, let no one separate" (Mark 10:9).

This book is dedicated with love, hope, and faith to my amazing God-fearing husband Jerry. To the beautiful women of faith, and the single women who strive to save themselves for marriage by committing to God wholeheartedly. To the couples in Christ, thank you for investing in your marriage and not giving up. Trust me, I know it seems like the easy thing to do but not by God's standards. It's always best to take the road less traveled and do things God's way. To the single women who are preparing for your future spouses, I pray you take heed to the instructions in this book as you discover the effectiveness of prayer and the power of God in every aspect of your lives. It is my prayer that each heart and marriage is submitted to Christ daily. By resisting the Devil and causing him to flee, you can be free to love and forgive your spouse just as God loves, and forgives you.

TABLE OF CONTENTS

PREFACE

"Though one may be overpowered by another, two can withstand him; and a threefold cord is not quickly broken" (Ecclesiastes 4:12, NKJ)

You can't change your husband. If you attempt to do so, you will fail miserably. But God cannot fail. You should love and aspire to honor your husband, especially if he is a godly man. Good godly men are hard to come by these days. It is imperative that you recognize your husband's strengths and remind him of them every chance you get, even when you don't feel like it. In doing so, you will build his confidence, and encourage him to draw closer to Christ – how invigorating! You will witness first hand as God helps him to become the man, leader, husband, and father that God intended him to be. Instead of stabbing him with criticism or pointing out his weaknesses, pray over him. Give the issues to God and watch what He will begin to do in your husband's life. Those weaknesses were not intended for you to foster or bear. He belongs to God first.

If your marriage is troubled and your husband is not the godly man you want him to be, you are still not excused from loving and respecting him. He is the man you took those sacred vows with at the altar before God. Look for the good treasures God placed within him. It may seem hard, but God makes the difference. You both have room to change and grow. Therefore, surrender and submit to God first. Then watch what God does in your marriage.

INTRODUCTION

1 have been a wife for more than half of my life, and I can tell you first hand that marriage is not a walk in the park or a race to the divorce court to solve problems. It is not always beautiful, but it can be interesting with beautiful God-like moments. It is more like a rollercoaster. You experience the highs and the lows.

There are moments of excitement that simply take your breath away while there are also sad moments that will make you wonder why you got married in the first place. However, the proportion of the highs to the lows depends on you. Your marriage is what you make it. It can be a boxing ring if you allow the Devil into it and refuse to check your behavior and that of your spouse. On the other hand, it can be a paradise if you constantly keep in touch with God through prayer and follow sound biblical marriage advice and principles.

I am not the best wife, and I'm not even close to being a perfect wife, so don't think that I am writing this book from a position of perfection. I am just a good wife in progress. I am continuously learning and listening to God for direction to understand my husband's weaknesses and strengths. The truth is human behaviors constantly change. You will never know it all but if you have a progressive mind and listen to the voice of God, you will continue to have a happy home. The wisdom of God will point you in the right direction.

The reason people get married in the first place tells a lot about where the marriage is headed and if it's going to survive or not. Did you get married for the sex? Because you have to do it on a regular basis? Or because you think that is what married couples do? Did you marry for the security? Or is it because you don't want to ever work a day in your life? Were you just lonely and needed someone to talk to every now and then? Were you under pressure to hook up with someone because all your friends are married? These are the wrong reasons to get married. It's not "better to marry than burn."

Nevertheless, if you have married for the wrong reason(s), there is still hope for you. In this book, I am going to share my thoughts and knowledge on what I know works in building a successful marriage. You will receive sound advice and learn time-tested principles that will make your home a happy one where peace and tranquility reign. I will equip you with the tools to be a good wife, to support your husband and also teach you how not to be a good knife stabbing him. It is my hope that you will find this work very useful for your marriage as the principles have worked for mine and many other successful marriages. Happy reading!

Chapter 1

Your Role as a Wife

*B*eing a good wife goes beyond keeping your end of the marriage contract you signed at the court or the church in front of many witnesses including God. It is more than just saying, "I do" to the list of promises read to you at the altar. It's more than the fairy tale wedding with all the bells and whistles you dreamed of as a little girl. Perhaps, you can't wait to broadcast and post your big day all over social media.

You will soon learn that marriage isn't for show and tell, unless God is the show stopper! In a marriage, your role as a wife extends far beyond what you agree to by law and in the presence of people. It is not typical for the presiding pastor to ask you whether you agree to pray for your husband, cook for him, clip his scrubby toenails, bring him back to Christ whenever he's going astray or when his testosterone is low and emotions are high. He most likely will not ask if you will respect him even when you are not sure he's making the right decision.

But in your heart, you know that as a wife, these are your roles; these are the things that you need to do if you want to have a successful home, and to build your marriage on a solid foundation. You must also know that your role even transcends loving him.

Unlike what you may think, love is not enough to sustain a marriage. You must go extra miles to make your husband happy and keep your home together. Your role in the family is a pretty serious, delicate, dynamic, and extremely important one. Many times, you have to be the coach and the player. Don't get me wrong; when I say "player," I don't mean the adulterous player having an affair. What I do mean is that you will need to be the captain, stay on top of the situation, and change tactics as often as it becomes necessary.

To be a good wife, you will need to perform certain functions and possess traits that will assist you in handling the everyday demands and several issues when they arise.

In this chapter, we are going to talk about a few of these functions so that you are well able to build a mutually satisfying relationship with your husband that will fulfill his needs, strengthen him and create a happy home you both will enjoy.

One of your most important roles as a wife is that of being a builder. Whether you agree with it or not, a woman performs the role of the coordinator of the home more often than a man does. As a wife, and a good one at that, you are expected to use your wisdom and the direction you get from God to build your home into a solid fortress where every member of the family feels loved and protected.

Your role as a wife is more important than your role as a mother. The role of a mother is critical, but it grows from being more of a "help meet." This does not mean that a single woman is incomplete and not important to God. If God asks an adult woman to remain single for a season or permanently in a special way, He becomes her husband. A single woman, "careth for the things of the Lord, that she may be holy both in body and in spirit" (1 Cor. 7:34).

Your role is to build a sanctuary, a safe haven (with the help of your husband, of course) to which your kids want to return and your husband wants to run. Knowing that most men are usually comfortable playing the role of the provider, the onus is left to you to take up the role of the builder and construct the kind of home you want for yourself.

One of the ways you can do that is to compliment your husband and avoid criticizing him privately, and in front of other people. Learning to compliment your husband is an essential element to having a successful marital relationship. It builds his self-esteem and will make him appreciative of your efforts. If you have children, you are also expected to join your husband in raising children with good, sound morals. Remember, your children are taking a front row seat, and you're the main act. How will it play out?

Wives also should understand and appreciate that there are certain legitimate needs and expectations husbands have within the marriage. One such expectation is that he will be satisfied sexually. As a wife, you should understand this and respect the sanctity of matrimony. For many men, sex can be likened to physical hunger, which needs to be filled. If the woman ignores this reality and her husband's needs, the relationship suffers.

Your role is to understand his needs from his perspective, not from yours. Even though it is also very important for your husband to respect your sexual needs, you also must understand and acknowledge the role of sex in your marriage and the fact that your husband might crave it much more than you do (ah breathe).

Sex is a gift; with it, you express your love to each other with God in the center. After all, God created sex for a man and woman to unite in more ways than one. Yes, God created sex, not man! Why would He not be at the center of this matrimonial bliss He designed just for the two of you to experience? Well, I will let you and your husband fill in the intimate details between the sheets (Bible sheets included) because who needs batteries when you have Jesus?

I pray you are including Jesus in this magic boom, boom room because He is the spark when the two of you light the match. I know you may not want to think about or bring God into your love affair, but don't allow the enemy to deceive you. God is the Creator of you and sex too.

There is nothing unknown, unseen, or unheard by God. He knows your body, and your hot spots. Therefore, you should communicate with Him about everything.

As a good wife, you must also radiate pleasantness. No one wants to be with someone who has a toxic attitude. You should be that one person in the family whom everyone comes to for peace. I don't mean a piece of your mind either. You need to be pleasant to yourself first. See yourself in a positive light and then try to beam this light on your family.

Don't be the kind of person who must transfer aggression to everyone just because you are having a bad day. It's not going to be easy, but it can be done. If you can't be pleasant most of the time, then make the decision not to suck your husband into your disagreeable behavior.

This applies to raising your kids as well. Yes, you are

allowed to discipline them for wrongdoing, but you must not do so in anger. Rather, be pleasant and graceful when making them accept that discipline. Don't shout at them and make them tremble; you may end up doing more harm than good.

No one wants a lazy woman as a wife and certainly, not as a mother. If you are indolent and slothful, this is an aspect of your life you will need to change. You have to do better. When we know better, we do better, right? As a wife, you are a role model in the family. Your husband is watching and your children are studying you; they are slowly mirroring your character, especially your girls. And most of the time, how you lead depends on how they will follow.

The same goes for your husband. How you behave determines how he will respond. Therefore, it makes a lot of sense for you to be hardworking in your business, your career, and your home. It is inevitable that a wife who can't do chores or cook and can't find a way around it will have some marital problems. Also, if you can't keep your job or be successful in your business, you stand a high chance of having problems in your home.

A good wife knows how to play the role of a special adviser on all matters. She is to be a counselor giving her husband sound, biblical advice. Eve acted as a counselor, which was her role, but she gave Adam evil advice. Adam knew the advice was wrong, but he followed it anyway. The same thing happened with Ahab and Jezebel.

"There was never anyone like Ahab, who sold himself to do evil in the eyes of the LORD, urged on by Jezebel his wife. He behaved in the vilest manner by going after idols, like the Amorites the LORD drove out before Israel "(1 Kings 21:25).

As a counselor, a wife should be careful to maintain her relationship with God, and increase her knowledge of the Word of God. Wisdom is essential in building a peaceful home and a wife needs a lot of it.

A good wife knows the power of her words. She knows when to encourage. She knows when to keep quiet and let her husband make the decision. She knows how to cover her husband's shortcomings without anyone knowing about them. A good wife, through wisdom, can perform as the anchor and the propeller. In other words, she should know when to give her husband the push when he is reluctant to act and when to call him to order when he is out of line. Your role is to know how to respectfully disagree with him but still offer him your support despite your feelings.

A good wife also tries to acquire the knowledge and skills necessary to deal with in-laws, relatives, and neighbors. Dealing with them can be a very tricky part of your marriage to navigate. Your role as a wife is to get wisdom and understanding to manage your home.

In conclusion, a good wife plays the role of a prayer warrior. You have to be the spiritual mentor and the principal motivator for the family. If you want a more intimate communication pattern with your spouse, would it not be beneficial to develop a more intimate communication line of prayer with God, the Holy One who spoke life into you?

Have you seen one of the most popular & highly inspirational movies of 2015, War Room? If not, you should! It will open your eyes more clearly to the role of prayer in your family. Another one of my favorite reads, *The Power of a Praying Wife* by Stormie Omartian also comes in handy in this regard. By utilizing the amazing and effective power of prayer, your relationship with your husband can be deepened, and you can help him in the areas of decision-making, spiritual strength, his role as a father and husband and in your future as a family.

Chapter 2

He is Your Husband, Not Your Son

*M*any times, women are heard speaking to their husbands as if they were their moms – or worse. You will often hear things like, "Where did you keep those bills. I've told you several times that you have to keep the bills for me so I can know how much you are spending?" "It will certainly help if you get a better job that pays more so you know how it feels." "I feed you, do the laundry, sleep with you, make your dinner, and do everything under the sun. What do you really do?" or "Can I trust you to take care of our kids while I'm gone?"

On Reddit, a user named "Fran" (not her real name as Reddit users employ monikers) made a post she termed as "hamburger meat moment." She explained:

"I started pulling things out of the bag, and realized he'd gotten the 70/30 hamburger meat — which means it's 70 percent lean and 30 percent fat.

I asked, 'What's this?'"

" 'Hamburger meat,' he replied, slightly confused."

"'You didn't get the right kind,' I said. 'You got the 70/30. I always get at least the 80/20.'"

"He laughed, 'Oh. That's all? I thought I'd really messed up or something.'"

Fran didn't let go after this. She launched into a long rant about why her husband didn't care enough to know what she wants, didn't bother to read the labels, and didn't care to get knowledge about her hamburger meat.

Yes, she expressed herself and let it all out as many people would have advised. But in the end, she realized that she made a mistake because her ranting didn't sound like an expression of displeasure. It sounded like she was scolding a child. On the website, she posted, "The bottom line in all this is that I chose this man as my partner. He's not my servant. He's not my employee. He's not my child."

This true, no man wants to be treated like a child. Sure, you have the right to be angry with your husband when he doesn't act the way you want or if he acts in a way that is not expected of him. Out of frustration comes the tendency to be rude and disrespectful. So, you are forced to think that he won't get it if you don't point out his error and tell him to change. You are forced to think that you are the only cord holding the entire household together and if it wasn't for you, no one in the family will enjoy life the way they are currently doing. Beautiful, you don't have that much authority! You only have what God gives you. God is always the cord holding the family together. It takes a husband, wife (you) and prayer as a whole to maintain unity.

But take a break. We all know you are a supermom and super wife even though it may appear as if your husband doesn't know this. Have you thought about the impact of your words when you are "speaking your mind?" Every time you mention his failures, every time you remind him that he has fallen short repeatedly, it sounds as if you are scolding a child.

Many times, you may be the problem. You are overwhelmed with child care, chores, bill payments and decision-making. However, very soon, you will discover that you are the one doing almost everything. And then, you look to find your help mate but he is not available. Do you want to know why? Because you didn't give him the room to do so. You put him on the backburner like the kids. You have strapped him to the backseat and shut him up with a pacifier. He dares not say anything as you drive the family around the way you want. He dares not say anything because you are the one who does everything. You are responsible for the family. Stop! You need to allow him to take responsibility for some things even if you are not comfortable with him doing so. Trust his ability to take the right decision even if it is something that you know he is not so good at. How will he improve if you do not give him a chance and trust him to do it?

Your man doesn't need two mothers, because guess what? Even one is too much to handle. He needs you to sit beside him, love him, trust his judgment, help him grow, and encourage him.

If your husband has grown very comfortable with being on the backburner, there is still hope for him. He will still take the offer of being in control in as much as you trust him to take you to the right destination. Sure, it may be scary trusting your husband to change your toddler's diapers and to watch over your other kids. But understand that if you don't give him the opportunity, you'd never know how well he can function. Your mistrust and fear might just be for nothing. After all, they're his children too.

Understand that God instructs your husband to lead the family. Therefore, He will teach him to if he's ready to listen. Yes, you know, but what if your husband is just not ready to lead? This is where you have to trust God wholeheartedly, and do your best to make sure that the backseat becomes inconvenient and uncomfortable for your husband. Tell him to handle the bills and get groceries while you take care of the laundry. If he makes mistakes, try to be forgiving and understanding. Don't nag him when he fails. God is forgiving. I'm sure you have made plenty mistakes as well! Lastly, go to God on your knees and ask Him to show you how to be more understanding. Ask Him to teach you how to be the type of wife your husband needs, not the second mother he doesn't need. Remember, prayer and faith work if you do!

If you have allowed your husband to relinquish his responsibility, think again. Sometimes, you need to take serious actions that will make him realize that his role is not to be a follower. God will give you the wisdom to act but you must also be willing to take actions. If you notice that your husband is not a self-starter in your marriage, refrain from treating him like a child by complaining or scolding him. Instead, deliberately leave gaps for him to fill.

If he is a smart man, he will see the void and know that it is his duty to fill it. If he doesn't see it, then you will have to be spontaneous. For example, you may need to get groceries while you are still nursing your baby but your husband doesn't look like he's going to help. The solution is pretty simple – go grocery shopping and leave your baby in the sitting room with him. Of course, you don't need to make the announcement that you are going grocery shopping. If you do, he may want you to take the baby with you. Call him when you are already in the car and tell him to look after the baby. If he protests, remind him that as the father, he also has a responsibility to take care of the child. Talk to him respectfully and politely and tell him where the diapers are. By the time you come back, he would have learned a thing or two about taking care of babies without you two having a quarrel. Moreover, the next time, he wouldn't be as helpless.

So, the next time you are tempted to treat him like he's your son, pause, take a step back, and pray. Look for better ways to make what you want come to life.

Chapter 3

His Money is Your Money

(He is not your Competition)

*F*rom the time money was adopted as the universal means of exchange, it has been the cause of many disagreements, strife, coups, and even murders. It is not surprising to see couples bickering over money more than they do over sex. Money can make a marriage sweet in the same way it can make it taste sour. But at the end of the day, the outcome is determined by how the people in the marriage decide to deal with money matters.

The Money is Mine, Not Yours

Often times, when couples are unable to agree on a financial plan, they split all the bills equally. As soon as the bills are sorted, each person is free to spend their income as they deem fit. On the surface, it looks like a reasonable plan. However, in reality, it isn't. Why do I say this? What a plan like this does is create feelings of resentment and jealousy over individual purchases. If your partner earns

$90,000 per year, and you earn just a little over $50,000, it may seem to be disadvantageous to the partner who earns less if both of you are sharing the cost of the bills equally. The low earner may feel that the partner with the higher salary can still afford a luxurious life while he /she can only dream of having one. This kind of plan reduces your spending power and removes a lot of the financial value that you are both supposed to enjoy as couples.

Have Common Plans and Goals

Instead of splitting bills into equally and spending the remainder of your income individually, you need to understand that after you took those sacred vows at the altar, the two of you became one. Included in your oneness is your finances. You should have a common goal and financial plan. You should both sit down periodically and discuss your finances.

It does not matter what your financial situation is or how uncomfortable you may feel, dealing with money matters together will save you a lot of strain and stress in your marriage. Talking about your goals including retirement, let's you know what you are working towards as a couple and you can decide how you will reach the goals set.

If you want to buy a home, pay off debts or save for retirement, it helps that you sit down to analyze the financial commitment required. How much do we need to get there? How much can we pull together every month? Who should leave more? These are the questions you should ask and answer. It is only in rare cases that both partners in a marriage will earn the same income. Usually, one person earns more than the other, and one person will also have more financial burdens than the other. You will need a change of the mindset you had when you were single and operate as a married couple. You should focus on the reality that as long as you are one, you are a family; it doesn't matter who earns what. You earn as one family; you plan as one family, and you spend as one family.

Address All Issues

When it comes to money, dialogue is very important. You must always talk about your financial situation with your partner before and after tying the knot. If he has outstanding student loans and debts, you want to know about them. If you have other sources of income and financial obligations, he should know about them. If he has child support payments, he must not hide that. Hiding financial information can come back to bite both of you later. Many times, it does hurt seriously. Laying all your cards on the table will inform you how to adjust your spending and plan on making more money to meet your targets.

Know your husband's money mindset...and check yours also

Sometimes when couples fight over money, they aren't really fighting over money per se; they are just fighting their temperaments. Your husband might be angry that you are spending too much while you might think that your income supports your lifestyle. Meanwhile, what he is thinking about is the future. He may be worried that your current lifestyle might cause you both to go bankrupt in the future. To better understand your spouse, you might need to look at his history. How was he raised? Does he have poor parents? Do they talk about money in their home? What is his greatest fear when it comes to money? If you know the answer to these questions, you will be more comfortable seeing your husband as your partner, not your competition when it comes to money.

Put a Budget in Place

Another great way to keep the competition off your marriage is to put a budget in place. Create a household budget. This will let you know how much you will be spending on your home. It will also help you track your spending and prevent the disagreements that may occur when one or both of you are in the dark about where all the money you are bringing to the table is being spent or invested.

Allow Some Breathing Room

While lying or keeping secrets about big spending should be frowned upon. Equally toxic, is the micromanagement of marital finances. Having to present every detail or to report every purchase you make can lead to bigger emotional issues. If your husband wants to micromanage you, be open and let him know you don't think it's the best approach if he's demanding accountability. For this reason, it is important that in your financial plan, you both make room for discretionary purchases. Having to obtain permission from your spouse to buy every single thing is an unhealthy, untenable, and discomforting practice. It is particularly so when you have to defend the purchase of something that he does not endorse.

Be Careful of Power Play

Power play happens in situations where your husband works and you don't, or you work and he doesn't. Situations like these tend to create rifts with the person who makes the most money dictating the terms of spending and the priorities. Although, the thinking behind this might be understandable, it is better if you operate as a team, rather than individuals. As a matter of fact, in marriage the two become one. Therefore, the decisions you make should include both partners as you are working towards the same goal. If not taken seriously, power play can build feelings of resentment.

For example, if you are unemployed, you might hate it when your husband tells you how much to spend on clothes and personal expenses because it makes you feel inferior. But if you are earning more than he does, you also need to be careful how you behave. You should avoid saying and doing things that will develop feelings of resentment in him. When married couples choose to separate the money, eventually, it separates the marriage.

The two of you vowed to be a team (united efforts achieve more), not solo artist with benefits.

Chapter 4

What's Your Husband's Love Language?

*Y*ou may have probably heard that the best way to love someone is to love them the way they want to be loved. You should also not love them the way you think they should be loved or the way that is convenient for you. According to Dr. Gary Chapman in his book, "The 5 Love Languages", there are five different ways people usually receive and send love.

The five love languages are: Quality Time, Words of Affirmation, Acts of Service, Physical Touch, and Receiving Gifts. Now, the question is: "Are you loving your husband the way that he wants to be loved?" Being able to learn, understand, and mirror your husband's love language will make your connection stronger.

The first step in finding your husband's love language is to establish how he receives love. Both of you can take a love language test at www.5lovelanguages.com. If he isn't willing to take the test, that's no problem. You can still get a good idea of his primary love language. You just have to be very observant. Look very carefully at how he expresses his love, what he complains about the most, and what kind of loving behavior he usually requests.

By default, we send love in our primary love language. For instance, if your primary love language is words of affirmation, you may show love to your husband by always making verbal reinforcement about your love to him, how much you value him, and how you will always love him. This is how you will know your love language. But if your husband's love language is not words of affirmation but acts of service, he may not really see a lot of meaning in your words. He might just see your words as words women say. However, don't get discouraged. You can show love to your language by carefully analyzing him using the strategy called mirroring.

Mirroring requires thoughtfulness and practice. Get a legal pad and look at some ways you can show love in your husband's language. Then proceed by carrying out a loving act every day to see how he reacts. For instance, to test if his love language is an act of service, make him a lovely dinner early that will take him by surprise. See how he responds. If that is his love language, he will be elated and will be over the moon. But there is a caveat. When you start trying to send love in a language that isn't primarily yours, it may not feel very natural but forced. Mirroring your husband's love language might require some extra effort, similar to learning how to speak Icelandic.

You can use the following as a guide:

Love Language: Words of Affirmation

Communicating it: Encourage him; affirm your love and commitment; appreciate him and empathize with him.

Recommended action: Send him an unexpected note, SMS, or hand-made card in the middle of the day. Encourage genuinely and do it more often that you usually do.

What to Avoid: Criticisms that aren't constructive, and not recognizing or appreciating his effort.

Love Language: Physical Touch

Communicating it: Employ the use of body language and use touch to show love and commitment. It doesn't have to always lead to sex.

Recommended action: Hug and kiss him when he least expects it. Hold his hands when walking beside him. Display physical affection more often and give some priority to intimacy.

What to Avoid: Physically neglecting him for long periods, leaving for a long period without intimacy, and receiving affection coldly.

Love Language: Receiving Gifts

Communicating it: Be thoughtful. Put him on your top priority list and speak to him with purpose.

Recommended Action: Go out of your way to get him gifts whether an occasion calls for it or not. Sometimes, small gestures matter in big ways. If he gives you a gift, show your appreciation.

What to Avoid: Not remembering special occasions.

Love Language: Quality Time

Communicating it: Make your conversation focused and uninterrupted. Spend time together one-on-one.

Recommended Action: Do well to create special moments with him, go on dates with him and cherish the special moments together. Plan to spend a special weekend alone with him.

What to Avoid: Distractions when you are spending time with him.

Love Language: Acts of Service

Communicating it: Employ phrases like, "I will" and "I'll help out with..." so that he will know that you are with him.

Recommended Action: Do things together; make him breakfast in bed and go out of your way to help relieve him of the stress.

Avoid: Pushing his request to the backburner while making other people high on your list of priorities.

Keep On Pushing On

You might not get his primary language in the first few days of trying, but he will definitely appreciate your gestures. The results may also not be immediate. However, most husbands tend to respond in like manner to your gestures when they see the efforts you are making. Don't rush the process to see the progress. It will happen in God's perfect timing. Just continue to be genuine, more so than expecting. Give him good feedback when he reciprocates your gestures.

If you make mirroring his love language an important and daily priority in your marriage, you will start to notice improvements in your husband. He will feel more secure and accepted in your relationship. The best aspect of mirroring love languages is that you both show love in ways that are meaningful to each other.

Notes

Chapter 5

Respect His Reputation

(Don't Air Your Dirty Laundry)

*M*any women are very good at pointing out the failures of their husbands while also punishing them for failing to meet their needs. It is not uncommon for these women to discuss their marital issues with their friends, in church, workplaces, yoga club, and even in gym class. But airing your family's case in the court of public opinion will not solve any problems for you. Far from that, it may create more issues.

Letting so many people into your marital affairs means that they will all have different views and perspectives. Unfortunately, some of the advice given can do more harm to your marriage than good. It can create problems and heartaches that you never had in the first place.

Don't tell your friends that you are the one paying the bills. That's none of their business. Instead of disrespecting your husband, nagging, yelling, and belittling him, why not treat him with respect by calmly communicating your issues to him? Why don't you just treat him like the king that he is. Hopefully, he will see your efforts and reciprocate.

Rather than thinking that he must earn your respect first, why don't you just show him respect without any requirement on his part? Watch him rise to the occasion by being the person God has designed him to be. "Nevertheless, let each one of you so love his own wife as himself, and let the wife see that she respects her husband" (Ephesians 5:33).

You must understand that it is your primary responsibility to respect your husband whether you think he deserves it or not. God commands wives to respect and submit to their husbands. This is a highly important principle to follow if you want a successful marriage. In our liberal societies today the roles of spouses are becoming blurred and the marriage as an institution is eroding at a rapid pace.

So how do you respect your husband? Treat him in a VIP manner! What does this mean? Treat him with respect verbally, intellectually, and physically.

Verbally

If your aim is to have a peaceful and happy marriage, then you must learn how to compliment your husband.

Compliments work like glue; they attract your husband to you even more. If you want to see improvement in a certain behavior, compliment him. You will find the behavior you desire will be amplified. Make it a practice to compliment him at least once every day. If you are finding it difficult to think of anything to compliment him on, think about what attracted you to him in the first place. Was it his physical features, mental ability, financial capability, strong relationship with other people (kids, friends, or parents)? Something must have attracted you to him to make you want to marry him.

At this point, you might probably be thinking, "But hey, why should I compliment him? He hardly even does that to me. He hardly tells me thank you even though I do the most important work in the house." That may be true. But you must understand that your husband is human. He probably doesn't even realize how much you value his compliments. This is why you should show kindness and give him encouragement. If he notices that you are praising him more often than you used to, he may be encouraged to appreciate you more for the roles you are playing in the family. Don't give up!

If there's a difficult issue that is bothering you, which you need him to act on, bring it up while you compliment him. For example, "Sweetheart, I know how hard you work to keep us where we are financially, but I need your answer on the mortgage matter tomorrow. I know it is expensive, but I trust that you will make a wise decision and let me know about it as soon as possible."

If the situation is extremely difficult and has even caused a breakdown of communication between you, it is important that you pray to God and then seek professional advice. Talk to someone you can trust not to spill out your family affairs. A marriage counselor is a good choice. Avoid telling your friends, coworkers, and gym class buddies about the issues you are facing in your family. If you are not careful, your family affairs will become a water cooler affair and a fodder for gossips.

Intellectually

Another good way to respect your husband is to appeal to his intelligence and his inclination towards problem-solving. Instead of saying, "Babe, this storage area is a mess with all your camping gear and sports stuff. I have so much to do and can't add this to my platter. Please get rid of all this junk!" you can say, "Babe, I need your help with clearing the storage area. Can you help me figure out a way to take out all those things you don't need so we can have more room for other stuff?"

Instead of saying, "I don't know how you could reason like that" say, "I don't understand your point, please make me understand." Seek his help on spiritual issues as well. If you do not understand a passage of scripture, seek his help. You will be surprised at what you will learn. If he isn't the spiritual leader in your home, go on your knees and continue to pray for him constantly. Don't go around telling people that your husband is spiritually weak, and you are the prayer warrior. It puts him in a bad light.

Men tend not to put a lot of importance on feelings. However, when you present the facts, they are more likely to come to order. For instance, if your husband wants to buy an expensive sports car at a time when you are in financial debt, don't launch into a long rant about why his decision is unreasonable.

A better alternative is to write a long list of expenses and tell him to choose what needs to be chopped off for him to buy his car. He will be more likely to follow your line of reasoning after seeing this. Let your fact speak, not your emotions. If it is impossible for you to reach a decision, don't go telling your mom about it or nag continuously for the remainder of the month. Honor his decision and let him continue to carry the family's responsibility.

Physically

Know what his needs are physically. It may not be easy to keep up with them because you also have your needs and have a life just as he does. Ask him what he wants, instead of asking your friends what they think men generally want.

Your husband is special and unique. You should not judge his needs by those of others. They may be at variance with what your husband wants. Look out for his body language especially when you are in public. Avoid communicating disrespectfully by rolling your eyes, crossing your arms, and slamming doors when in public. Let your actions show your love.

In conclusion, understand that respect is a verb as well as a noun; it is an attitude. Therefore, you should let the respect for your husband reflect in your thoughts, deeds, words, and actions. He will be more willing to give you love and affection if he is respected and admired. At first, he might be skeptical about your adjusted attitude but your commitment to treating him nicer can turn the table around and make him love you differently. To end it all, ask God for his strength as you are trying to obey his words. "I can do all things through Christ who strengthens me" (Philippians 4:13).

Chapter 6

Don't Compete – Be His Helpmeet

*F*rom time to time in marriage, couples engage in fire-for-fire competitions with each other. This behavior is unappealing. It creeps into their lives, takes over the couple, and rips the joy and love in a marriage apart. Competition is neither healthy nor fun, but some way, somehow, in the best of marriages, couples compete whether consciously or unconsciously.

To the detriment of the relationship, we are concerned about who earns more. Chances are that if you earn more as a wife, you are proud of your achievements. When you realize that you may have to shell out more money for the family expenses, it soon becomes a problem. You start to brood over your new situation.

The competition becomes so fierce that if your husband makes a bigger bonus or gets a promotion, you start to subconsciously think about why he got a raise, and you didn't when in fact, you work harder than he does – at home and at work. If he is planning to get a second degree, you also want to get into the race so that you don't get left behind in your career.

In church, you compete if he becomes the head of a committee within a few months of becoming a member while you have been a member for years without any form of recognition. If the kids love spending more time with him than they do with you, you start feeling bad because it seems like they are not appreciative of your efforts — you have invested more time, money, and emotions. Yet, they run off to meet Dad who spends half of the time at work. The list is endless and this feeling of competition could be dangerous if left unchecked.

Any couple who allows competition to take a foothold in their marriage will create a breeding ground for the activities of the enemy. Competition creates envy and makes room for it. It causes division and deviates the marriage from the way God intended.

The source of marital competition is insecurity. Surprisingly, trust in marriage is built on the security of both partners. But competition removes the security and trust in the marriage. You purpose is not to outperform your husband. Rather, you should make each other shine, grow, and become better together.

In Genesis 2: 4, it says that "Two shall become one flesh."

Husbands and wives are to work together as a single unit. Jesus said in Matthew 19:6 that, "What God has joined together, let no man put asunder." A competing mindset creates separation instead of unification. When you compete with your husband, you are making yourself look better and emasculating your husband.

In Ephesians 5, Paul admonished the church to "Submit to one another in the fear of Christ." He also admonished wives to submit (or show respect) to their husbands and for husbands to love their wives even as Christ loved the church and gave Himself for her.

You shouldn't try to outclass your mate (the same goes for your husband too). Your duties are to serve one another in love and help each other succeed at goals. As you lift each other up, instead of comparing and competing, you will experience growth and happiness in your marriage. As you work to build each other's self-esteem, security and trust will be built and competition will fade away. That is the way marriage was designed by God.

The overarching purpose of marriage is to give God glory. The Bible does not in any way encourage you to compete with your spouse for anything. What it does is advocate love and understanding. Therefore, you should always root for each other, encourage one another to grow, and build each other up. When you do this, you will see that the desire to compete with your spouse will fade away.

Another way you can be a helpmate for your partner is to always pray for him. This is extremely important. Pray concerning any difficulties, he is experiencing or that you are both experiencing. Pray for wisdom to navigate your challenging journeys successfully. Let prayer precede any thoughts or action. Pray without ceasing.

If your husband is experiencing any problems, your responsibility is to help lighten his burdens. And ask him to reciprocate the support if you are in his shoes. Who wants to come home after having a bad day at work losing a top investor to take out the trash, pick up the dry cleaning or call the cable company? When you help lighten his burden, he will love and appreciate you for it.

If your husband feels insecure and tries to compete with you, reassure him that you are both in this race together, and he shouldn't see you as the enemy. Rather, he should see you as the friend he needs and deserves. Let your love for him overlook his mistakes, faults, and insecurities. If he is stressed out or something is easily upsetting or irritating him, give him the time and space he needs to work through the issue. But be ready to shower him with grace and forgiveness.

In cases where he has messed up and made mistakes, don't stir the pot or rehash and nag about his discrepancies. Let your actions be for healing and peace. Do whatever you can not to regurgitate your feelings of anger because of the hurt and unfair treatment he may have meted out to you in the past. Focus on moving forward with the hope of a better life together.

If you do not support your husband's ideas, you don't have to pretend that you do. Disagree gracefully and respectfully. If he doesn't back down and wants to move on with the execution of his plans, don't stop him. Offer your support in whatever way you can. Don't be the negative voice that stands in the way of his dreams.

<u>Notes</u>

Chapter 7

Respect His Manhood

(God made you the weaker vessel for a reason)

*W*e are all created equal before God. This applies to marriage also. However, God made man and woman with an overlapping set of needs. He created marriage so that the husband can meet his wife's needs and the wife can meet her husband's needs. For men, one of the most important needs is respect and honor. They cannot meet these needs themselves. Someone else must provide them.

Paul, in the book of Ephesians 5:33 advised women to respect their husbands. He didn't say respect your husband the way your mom did. He didn't even mention respecting your husband the way the wife of your spiritual leader does. And nowhere in the Bible was it written that you should respect your husband the same way you see it done on TV. Following the lifestyles, you see on television creates chaos, confusion, and will have you divorced before the next reality show airs. Beautiful? Those fantasy shows are full of air and a whole lot of airbrushing. They're role-playing and acting. The Bible says that you should respect your husband. That's all! It is not conditional. It is a commandment and great advice.

And if you are observant, you will notice that men are generally attracted to the places where they are honored and respected. If work fills your husband's needs, he will spend more of his time there and work himself to a stupor. If his needs are not satisfied at home, he will come home late at night and leave very early in the morning so he doesn't have to deal with disrespect. Before your feet can hit the floor, your husband is out the door.

Does this sound like your marriage? Be honest. It's just you, God, and this book. If you do not respect him and another woman at work does, who do you think he will be drawn to? Intentionally or unintentionally, you don't want to contribute to his infidelities or vulnerabilities at all.

We must be careful as wives to create an environment that allows us to confront any issues or concerns freely. Avoid criticism, it benefits no one. Always put the caring wardrobe on that says, "I care how you feel, think, and what your heart must say to me." Without confronting our concerns, but holding them in by "sweeping them under the rug," we create a volcanic explosion that destroys everything in its path!

As women, we can get cranked up in two minutes and create a love affair in three seconds. Smile because you know it's the truth, not because you think it's cute (it's not). Your husband may walk in thirty minutes late and you ask, "Where you been?"

He replies, "I ran into Tommy at Jimmy's shop and we got to talking."

You reply, "Tommy, who is Tommy?"

Before he can respond you snap and say, "Don't play me for no fool, you meant Tammy, and why she twerking for you?"

He responds, "The only Tammy I been with is the one inside your head, and the only thing twerking is your mouth."

"Oh, so you calling me stupid?"

Baby what is bothering you? Girlfriend, you are still stuck on Tammy because of your insecurities or his lack of affection. Get to the source of the problem, don't add fuel to the fire by creating something that's not there. Don't make accusations unless you have solid evidence.

One of the best ways to respect your husband is to allow him to fail. You are shocked, right? This is it; men are humans like you. They are not gods. This means they make mistake. Sometimes, you must let them make these mistakes. Don't damage your marriage or disrespect him by telling him what to do all the time. Don't treat him like a toddler. It is not your duty.

Failure is an opportunity to learn. Failure is an opportunity to find out what doesn't work so that when you eventually do what works; you can increase your self-esteem. You can respect him by allowing him to be independent and make his mistakes. Of course, don't allow him to wallow in depression, but let him find himself; it is part of being a man.

Most men generally like dictating the terms in most situations, and it's perfectly alright if you don't agree with what he does or says sometimes. After all, you are both equals. But when you register your disagreement, leave it at that. Don't go whining and nagging. Instead, pray that God directs his heart to do the right thing.

Honor the man you want him to be. If you want him to be the kind of man you want, start treating him like that. Let him see it by your actions. As you respect him, he will be proud of you and respect you as well. Look at what you first saw in him and where you want him to be. Then start treating him at that level and watch him rise to the challenge.

If you approach your husband with an issue or something

on your heart, and he says, he doesn't feel like talking, set up a time to talk. Briefly, let him know what it's about. You may want to say it like this: "Honey, when you left the past two mornings, you didn't respond when I told you I love you. Is something bothering you? Is something wrong between us because I'm feeling hurt, and insecure." It is better to be real about how you feel than to fill your heart with anger or try to play you are a tough girl. I call it reverse psychology. Playing that game can have deadly effects and outcomes.

Work on your ability to respond rather than react. When you are communicating with him, try to listen more and be angry less. If you don't understand what is being communicated, ask questions for clarity. Arguing with him compounds the issue.

Allow your husband to take charge of the affairs at home. Put your trust in God. Ask Him to guide your husband to make sound decisions in the best interest of your family. Respect God as the head of the family. Let your husband call the shots and allow him make the final judgment when you are both bickering about something. At the end of the day, he will be held responsible by God for the consequences because God established him as the head of the family.

The enemy will press you to focus on your spouse's bad

qualities. But this is not what God wants. Too often, women complain about their husband's failures than their successes. But marriage grows in an environment of praise. Therefore, you should cover his faults and highlight his strengths. To do this successfully, you must evaluate your spiritual maturity and ask God to show you areas where you can improve.

Learning how to truly respect your husband requires a great deal of emotional and spiritual maturity, but God will stand with you every step of the way. Examine how you communicate with God and ask Him to be your guide. Ask Him to help you grow in all the areas you need improvement t and teach you to respect your husband.

As I said earlier, when your husband makes mistakes, try to show grace just as God does. Be more encouraging as opposed to being judgmental or critical. Tell God to help you refrain from judging or criticizing your husband and instead encourage him as often as you can.

When your husband sees that you are encouraging him, he will want to trust you and confide in you the more. And when he talks about his challenges, resist the urge to give him unsolicited advice. Many times, he will just want you to listen. Men always want to be men. They seek solutions on their own. If he doesn't ask, don't offer. Just listen. If he does, then you can use the opportunity to display the wisdom that God has given you.

In conclusion, pray every day about God's plan for your family. Pray daily that that the Holy Spirit renews your mind and disciplines you to focus your thoughts on what is true, noble, right, pure, lovely, admirable, and worthy of praise whatever the situation.

Notes

Chapter 8

Inspiration vs. Insecurity

*A*s a single unit, whenever there is a problem with one of you, it becomes a collective problem. It's similar to the human body. If your finger hurts, the entire body hurts. Perhaps, your husband used to be a self-starter, a go-getter who was always on top of every situation, but lately he doesn't want to do anything. He moves around the house with little effort or diligence. He doesn't want to help with the dishes or watch the kids. He is uninspired. Inevitably, because of your oneness, it starts to infect you.

You start to wonder if you have lost your husband to something you have not yet identified. Your marriage seems like you are the only one in it as of late. Should you feel insecure and get worried sick? No. What you should do is seek motivation for yourself and your husband. You need to find motivation in the Word of God. Find comfort in His words and trust in your ability to get out of the limbo.

No marriage is entirely filled with sunshine. There will

always be patches of gloom, sadness, and disappointment. This is reality. Your husband will not always feel lovey-dovey. You may come home from work irritated and angry and transfer your aggression to him. He may not be in the mood to deal with your attitude and things may quickly degenerate into chaos. You don't want that. So, the alternative is to find a way to inspire yourself and your spouse to rid your marriage of feelings of insecurity.

Your husband might have lost his glow due to problems at work. It could even be something you don't know about. In fact, it could be nothing. So, try not to feel insecure that something beyond your comprehension is happening. Also, if you are the one feeling zapped of energy, don't make your partner feel insecure.

The first step you should take after discovering you have a problem is to look at the cause. Is he feeling dull because he suffered a setback at work? Sometimes, the reason may not be that clear. It's Saturday, why is he not playing soccer with his friends? Why is he canceling date night? Talk to him. Communicate your feelings and the way his behavior is affecting you. Doing so may cause him to change. People react differently to events and circumstances.

Your husband might not want to bother you with his problems even though he is already bothering you with his behavior. Having a genuine conversation with him can help you lift his spirit. A heart-to-heart talk can assist in removing feelings of isolation and may lead to renewed motivation.

It makes sense if you initiate the conversation; this will be a plus for you. Talk about what's going on. See if you can both get things off your chest and if necessary, ask for his advice on how to get back on track. In life, a negative outlook can become a habit and when it does, it becomes too difficult to shake off. Half of the things we do daily we do as habits and, of course, habits grow into attitudes. Helping your husband identify the reasons why he's demotivated can help you get your motivation back on track. Help him replace complacency with optimism and enthusiasm to live a good life.

Sometimes, people may know the right direction but not the right steps to get there and where to start. In the case of your husband, this is where you come in. If he has a problem with his job, help him search for new leads. If he's overweight, make it a point to cook healthier meals. If he's going into isolation and doesn't want to see his friends, take the initiative of inviting them over for dinner and drinks. These little pushes might make him more proactive.

If he takes a positive step, offer him incentives so that he resumes the activities he is used to enjoying. If you want to go shopping but he doesn't, offer to treat him to his favorite lunch at his favorite restaurant and end the day at a late-night cinema.

Sometimes, you may have to raise the stakes. Some men are just competitive by nature. If you want to get him to spring into action, call another man to do the job. For example, if the kitchen sink needs fixing, don't tell him to do it. Just notify him that you have called a plumber. If he's someone with mechanical skills and a knack for fixing things, he will quickly spring to action and do the fixing himself. If he wants to quit drinking, show him someone who wants to do it in a month and pitch them together.

Encourage him to think positively. Let him know that his actions will lead to something good. If he realizes that people are passing snide remarks about your overgrown lawns, he will do something about it. If he knows that your kids are jealous of other kids because they have a father who is more present, he will change.

In conclusion, appreciate your husband's kind words and gestures. Boost his confidence when you are with other people. Squeeze his hands. Pat his back and make him look good in public. Compliment him; praise him without flattery, of course. Insincere sweet talk is not advised.

If you want your man to be up on his feet or do what you want him to do, he will need your motivation.

Chapter 9

Dealing with My Husband's Sin

*I*t is best to start this chapter with the understanding that we are all sinners and have fallen short of the glory of Christ Jesus. Irrespective of whom you marry, whether they are white, Hispanic, black, rich, poor or vegetarian, you are still bonded to someone who is imperfect. You are still bonded to someone who can only be saved by God's grace.

Because you are also not perfect, irrespective of how many Sundays' school classes you attend or the number of times you pray per day, you will also hurt him very badly. If you are married to a believer, you are in luck, but if you aren't, there is so much grace, mercy, and forgiveness at the feet of Jesus Christ for him.

Now, even though the Bible encourages you to submit to your husband, it doesn't say that you should accept his sins. The Bible doesn't say you should keep quiet and let him descend further into sin. Nonetheless, delicate issues like this need to be approached with great humility, respect, prayer, and the guidance of the Holy Spirit.

How can this be done? First, you must be sincere when communicating with him about his actions. If there's a sin he keeps on committing, it needs to be addressed. Do not let him continue in that sin by covering it up. Instead, show true love by confronting him gently and humbly. In Galatians 6: 1-2 and Matthew 18:15-18, we are all encouraged to confront our fellow believers about sin with love and humility; spouses are no exceptions.

Before you confront him and attempt to remove the speck in his eyes, seek the Lord first. In Matthew 7:1-5, the Bible tells us:

> Do not judge, or you too will be judged. For in the same way, you judge others, you will be judged, and with the measure you use, it will be measured to you. "Why do you look at the speck of sawdust in your brother's eye and pay no attention to the plank in your own eye? How can you say to your brother, 'Let me take the speck out of your eye,' when all the time there is a plank in your own eye? You hypocrite, first take the plank out of your own eye, and then you will see clearly to remove the speck from your brother's eye.

Spend time in prayer and supplication. Seek the face of

God for direction before you engage him in conversation. Let your desire to confront him come from a place where you seek his spiritual restoration, and not from your desire to "fix" things. Look inward to see where there are areas of sin in your life that need to be confessed to God and maybe even your husband (Matthew 7:5). It might not be easy, but you will need to extend the arm of grace, which you have received from God when confronting your husband.

As you plan to confront him, purge your mind of unrealistic expectations. Look to the Holy Spirit to help convince him, rather than your own words. Once this has been done, depend on the Holy Spirit to bring conviction. Don't stress the issue any longer; leave the matter to God to settle and take total control.

If after all the conversations and prayers, he is still unrepentant, you can take the strategy a notch higher. Read Matthew 18:15-18 and act on the instructions outlined therein. The book of Proverbs 27:5 reads that, "Better is open rebuke than love that is concealed. Faithful are the wounds of a friend."

You must also forgive him whether he shows remorse or not. "If your brother sins, rebuke him, and if he repents, forgive him. If he sins against you seven times in a day, and seven times comes back to you and says, 'I repent,' forgive him (Luke 17:3-4).

The Bible teaches that if a believer sins against us and shows repentance, we must forgive him/her. If you do not do this, God will not forgive you. If you can see yourself as someone who is in need of grace and mercy from the Lord, then you will learn how to show mercy to other people.

Chapter 10

Withholding Sex is a Sin

The book of 1 Corinthians 7:1-5 (Message version) reads:

First, is it a good thing to have sexual relations? Certainly—but only within a certain context. It's good for a man to have a wife, and for a woman to have a husband. Sexual drives are strong, but marriage is strong enough to contain them and provide for a balanced and fulfilling sexual life in a world of sexual disorder. The marriage bed must be a place of mutuality— the husband seeking to satisfy his wife, the wife seeking to satisfy her husband. Marriage is not a place to "stand up for your rights." Marriage is a decision to serve the other, whether in bed or out. Abstaining from sex is permissible for a period of time if you both agree to it, and if it's for the purposes of prayer and fasting—but only for such times. Then come back together again.

Satan has an ingenious way of tempting us when we least expect it.

Many married women do not know that sex is a marital duty. They see it only as an avenue for their pleasure. It is your responsibility to have sex with your husband! One of the purposes of marriage is the fulfillment of sexual needs. When you are both satisfied sexually, you guard yourself against temptation. You are less tempted to seek sex outside of the marriage. A sexually satisfied person has a lower risk of having impure sexual fantasies and engaging in pornography and extra-marital affairs.

Paul, in his letter to the Corinthians warned that the Devil will try his best to destroy your marriage. As a woman, it is your calling to protect your husband, not because he is weak but because God has given you this task as a way of honoring him. By having sex, you are protecting his mind from impure thoughts as he will be thinking about you and how you will please him. Regular lovemaking will draw him closer to you because he knows you love him and are doing your best to make him feel loved.

Withholding Sex

When you withhold sex from your husband whether to threaten, punish or bribe him, you are committing sin. If you withhold sex without giving him a reason, you are also in danger of sin.

Many women usually give the excuse that they are too tired, too stressed, have a headache, don't feel comfortable and are too busy. But you have to know that these are not valid excuses.

If you are too tired, remember that this is your duty, and it's what you agreed to when you said, "I do" at the altar. Trust me; it was in the fine prints. True, there will be nights when you will feel too tired to have sex with your husband. But if this happens regularly, then you have to check your life and reevaluate what you are doing with your time.

Sex with your husband is a "must–have"; it should be factored into your schedule. If you are too overwhelmed with your daily activities, find a way to decongest and rework your schedule. Reanalyze where you are putting your energy so that you can have more time for sex. If you don't, someone else will. He will certainly get your attention then.

I admit, it's not so easy when you are a mom and have a 9 to 5 job. However, you must also realize that you married your husband, not your kids. Show him that you love him by needing him too.

If you are too busy, then un-busy yourself. Make your husband your top priority. Everything else can wait. Talk to him. Let him know what he can do to help with all the activities you have lined up. If he comes to you in a bid to help you out, allow him. Don't say he cannot do it the way you would. Yes, I've been there and sometimes, I've had to go back and regroup. I like things done a certain way. So, in order for my husband to partake in the chores or anything else, I had to relinquish my way of doing things. I had to be more open to the fact that he is not me, nor is anyone else who may lend a helping hand. Trust him to do it and if you can guide him, do that also. If you make yourself too busy, you won't have enough time to relax and enjoy your sex life.

If you are too stressed, tell your husband about what's stressing you. You never can tell; he might have the answer to your problem. Research has also shown that having sex releases endorphins and oxytocin, which activate pleasure centers in the brain.

Some women do not feel comfortable having sex. Many report that they experience pain during intercourse while others feel shy about being naked in front of their husbands. If you are experiencing pain during sex, seek professional help and let your husband know what is happening to you instead of denying him sex.

If have been raped or sexually abused, and it is negatively impacting your marriage, talk to a counselor as well as your husband. Seeking help can assist your healing process so you can meet your husband's expectations for sex in the marriage.

In conclusion, you need to pray about whatever decisions you make. Tell God to help you make better decisions and give you the wisdom and strength to follow through. If you really need to withhold sex, you should talk to your husband. Make sure that he agrees with your proposition. Set a time frame for how long you will be abstinent so that he knows what to expect.

You can show affection without having sex. Touch, kiss, and embrace each other frequently. Spend time together. Make your marriage and home sanctuaries of happiness and love so that even if you both agree to a period of abstinence, he still feels loved.

Don't Repay or Return Sin for Sin

Make up your mind that you will not follow the crowd, the opinions of your single girlfriends, or the coldness in your heart. Don't be quick to seek revenge without thought or reason. God's Word tells us not to repay evil for evil, but evil for good. So, what does this entail? For me, it means that as a wife, mother, sister or friend, I have to take full responsibility for my words, actions, and wrongdoings wholeheartedly. You're not responsible for the way other people treat you, but you're responsible for how you react and respond. Yes, I know what you're thinking and, "You're not weak." Truthfully, you're the weaker vessel when it comes to your spouse.

Does this mean you shouldn't be shown respect and love, of course, you should be respected? Just keep in mind that love and righteousness are greater than any evil. Never be too proud to say, "I'm sorry," or "I forgive you." Don't let your emotions get the best of you. I strongly encourage you not to go to bed angry and possibly awake to a deceased spouse. It can happen in the blink of an eye. Tomorrow isn't promised to any of us.

Your husband is supposed to be your better half. Having an unforgiving heart is like having a dead mouse inside your walls deteriorating. After a period of time, it will begin to stink up the entire house. In other words, un-forgiveness can and will eventually contaminate its surroundings and the people who reside there. God is very clear about the fact that he expects us to forgive others.

Most women are intensely interested in books, topics, chatrooms or conferences dealing with relationships and marriage because we play a vital role in our homes, communities, and societies. We desire to be part of the outside roles while juggling our domestic roles. It is great that you want to contribute outside the home, but what happens when you take away from your own home to provide for others? Your role in the domestic environment is just as important if not more important than in the society.

Women who are housewives and stay-at-home mothers are often viewed as "less than" to others in society because they're not career -centered. There is nothing wrong with being career-centered if you don't have a husband or children. But to those who do, something is always lost when you have to work outside the home, no matter how great the caregiver is. There will be some sort of guilt when you rely on caregivers to care for your children. I'm not saying you're a bad mother or wife if you have to work because you may have no choice.

But let's be real, your children and husband benefit more when you can give your attention fully to the home and their hearts. Your children are gifts from God, not accessories that don't accompany you. They're not clients you consult once a month. Many women today feel they need to make their own money. But when you get married, both of the incomes if there are two paychecks are supposed to be one bank account under, "God We Trust."

Why get married to just live separately? Once you start separating the ownership, you no longer are in a marriage. You are considered as friends with benefits and baggage. Before we can make progress in ourselves, and marriage we must submit to God's will first: "Submit yourselves, then, to God. Resist the devil, and he will flee from you" (James 4:7). We must learn that submission to God is important. It determines the success or failure of anything or anyone.

Far too often, we think we have a plan or solution to fix problems – our marriage being one of them. But this is just arrogance and pride working together making room for the enemy to come in and destroy homes. He breaks hearts that seep out like a plague destroying everything, and everyone crossing its paths. This is not the woman and wife God has called you to be.

Chapter 11

Don't Choose Luxury Over Love

*M*any of you may have godly, well- intentioned husbands who show their love by working long hours to provide for your families. In their eyes, providing for the family is their expression of love. Sure, you may get the lavish gifts: going on expensive trips, carrying the brand name purses and wearing the trendy shoes. You brag to the world and show and tell on social media just to fill the emptiness you feel when you see the couples who pray together, hold hands in public, and smile as they share intimate chats.

Or you may be one who has the affectionate husband, who cannot afford all the lavish trips, and gifts. Some women don't need these things to feel loved. They are looking for something more intimate. Some of us crave closeness to our spouses, others crave stuff. What we need most, more than all the expensive vacations in the world is simple, specific, day-to-day actions that show love.

Clearly, a few small actions won't fix deep-rooted relationship problems. But for most of us, they increase the chances that our spouses feel we care deeply about them, instead of feeling that we don't care. There's just enormous power in that act alone! We must be able to communicate this to our husbands daily, and reciprocate that same affection. Don't rob your husband of closeness because he's a man and you think he doesn't need it. Don't try to compete with the Jones and bankrupt your marriage, put a strain on your relationship or stress your husband out. Enjoy the simple things in life and leave the complicated stuff with Jesus!

Share What Matters to Him

My husband is a huge Tarheel basketball fan and Panther football fan. I never was a fan of either, other than cheering for my school's athletic teams in high school. Not because I don't like it but because I never understood it. So, my husband prefers that I watch the games with him. Let's just say, I would watch with him. But oh, boy! Let me tell you what that looks like. I get confused distinguishing between the first and ten, from the actual touchdown. It doesn't bother my husband a bit. He finds me to be funny in a loving way. We laugh, and I get to ask questions like, "Why do a bunch of grown men hit each other on the butts?" In the end, it deepens our relationship, friendship and intimacy.

Listed here are some scriptures that can be effective in helping you build your marriage and be a wife versus tearing it down and being a knife. When we digest and apply God's Word, we will be more apt to keep "short accounts" with offenses. That helps to build a strong foundation in your marriage with God at the center. So together, you and your husband should set a time to discuss your relationship with God's Word. This is not to point the finger or to blame anyone, but to listen respectfully to one another's hearts.

We identify the characteristics of love in 1 Corinthians 13:4-7:

Love is Patient

> ❖ Have you and your spouse been patient with each other?

> ❖ Do you bear with one another's weaknesses wholeheartedly?

> ❖ Do you allow each other to grow in God's timing?

Love is Kind

> ❖ Have you both been treating each other with loving kindness, and God's grace?

❖ Have you been compassionate in your attitudes, and actions?

❖ Have you been negative and critical vs. having a positive outlook?

❖ Have you been using sarcasm, and unloving words when you relate to each other?

Love Does Not Envy

Do either of you display a spirit of envy? What exactly is envy? It's when you want something someone else has. It is unlike jealousy, which is being afraid of losing something or someone to another.

❖ Have you or your soul mate been exhibiting discontentment or resentment in what you have or don't have with each other or your marriage?

❖ It does not boast; it is not proud

❖ Have you been boastful, and arrogant in your role and good deeds in the marriage?

❖ Are you displaying an attitude of superiority or being smarter than your spouse? What does it accomplish?

It is Not Rude

- ❖ Have we been rude, intolerant or harsh with each other?

It is Not Self-seeking

- ❖ Have you been living together in partnership not allowing our individual wants to take precedence over our relationship as a marital team in Christ?

- ❖ Do you serve your spouse more or expect to receive more from your marriage partner?

It is Not Easily Angered

- ❖ Have you been irritable, loose tempered or hypersensitive?

It Keeps No Record of Wrongs

- ❖ Are you keeping score of the past with each other?

- ❖ Are you keeping score of that which we shouldn't?

Love Does Not Delight in Evil but Rejoices in the Truth

- ❖ Have you been amusing yourself and taking delight in the things which do not please God?

- ❖ Have you been self-pleasuring to satisfy your wants

at the expense of your marital partner's needs?

❖ When you converse do you speak the truth in love?

It Always Protects

❖ Have you been protecting each other's feelings?

❖ Have you rudely embarrassed or belittled each other publicly and privately?

❖ Can it be in any way interpreted that you attack each other's characters?

Always Trusts

❖ Have you been personally living lives of trustworthiness before God and each other?

❖ Have you been putting your trust in Christ wholeheartedly that He can help you work through your problems?

❖ Have you believed the best of your spouse – that he or she has your best interest at heart?

Always Hopes

❖ Have there been times when you have been too quick to assume the worst in each other?

❖ Has it been evident that you have hope because of

Christ?

Always Perseveres

❖ Have you given up too easily on that, which you shouldn't?

❖ Are you persevering through problems and conflicts rather than caving into them?

"But among you there must not be even a hint of sexual immorality, or of any kind of impurity, or greed, because these are improper for God's holy people. Nor should there be obscenity, foolish talk or coarse joking"

(Ephesians 5:3-4).

Have you protected your marriage sexually in what you view, by not looking at sexual entertainment anywhere outside of your marriage bed?

Are you both going the "extra mile" to show trustworthiness, honoring your spouse and God by the way you interact with those of the opposite sex? Remember, you must put up protective hedges so there's not even a chance of anyone misunderstanding your words or your actions?

<u>Notes</u>

Chapter 12

Submission – Not My Cup of Tea

"Wives, submit yourselves to your own husbands as you do to the Lord" (Ephesians 5:22).

*I*n this verse, we're not asked, but commanded by God to submit to our husbands. Oh boy! I know what you're thinking or at least what society has broadcast and embedded in the minds of women all over the globe. They've taken the words "servant," and "helpmeet" and made them the synonyms of the word "slavery." Basically, implying you must serve your husband's every whim. But that's not the case. Why? Because the husband must be under submission to Christ and His Word.

You're not a slave, but a co-ruler with him. Think of it as co-signing a vehicle. You're helping him to build his credit rating. He needs you, and you need him. You're a team God designed to work together. Just remember when you fight against your husband you also fight against God's purpose for you, and His kingdom.

"Nevertheless, in the Lord woman is not independent of man, nor is man independent of woman. For as woman came from man, so also man is born of woman. But everything comes from God" (1 Corinthians 11:12).

Overall, God has the final say. As a wife, you must help your husband carry the weight that has been placed upon him. He can't bear it alone; that's why God gave him a helpmeet. Your role is to keep his electrical wires grounded or everyone who comes into contact with him will be shocked – including you. You both must stay plugged into God's Word.

What Happens if Your Husband is an Ungodly Man?

Sometimes, wives try to win their ungodly husbands to Christ by overly criticizing, "witnessing," trying to force them to go to church, etc. Loving submission – as to Christ – and a godly lifestyle are the best witnesses.

Only if the husband is committing an offense that has biblical grounds for divorce that becomes an option. "For the unbelieving husband is sanctified by the wife and the unbelieving wife is sanctified by the husband: else were your children unclean; but now are they holy" (1 Corinthians 7:14). "Likewise, ye wives, be in subjection to your own husbands; that, if any obey not the word, they also may without the word be won by the conversation [Old English for entire lifestyle] of the wives" (1 Peter 3:1).

Here are some questions you and your spouse can write down, then exchange and review in love. Remember to be understanding, loving, and sympathetic to each other's hearts. Allow the Holy Spirit to guide you, and speak so you can avoid chaos, strife or confusion.

The goal is to be a wife not a knife. Don't forget to fight him with prayer. It works! Put your faith in God and each other. Honor God by working as a team not as enemies at war. The only war room you should have is the one that fights for the marriage, not against it. The focus here is about starting from where you are, not where you were. You both are better for it.

Reflecting on Ways to Better your Marriage.

Answer, and exchange these questions with each other in truth and love.

1. What can I do to make my husband/wife feel more loved?

2. What can I do to make my husband/wife feel more respected?

3. What can I do to make my husband/wife feel more understood?

4. What can I do to make my husband/wife more secure?

5. What can I do to make you feel more confident in our future direction?

6. What attribute would you like me to develop?

7. What attribute would you like me to help you develop?

8. What achievement in my life would bring you the greatest joy?

9. What would indicate to you that I really desire to be more Christ-like?

10. What mutual goal would you like to see us accomplish?

Positive Affirmations

❖ Every day I am more loving toward by spouse as Christ is towards me.

❖ Every day I fall in love with my wife/husband all over again.

❖ Every day my marriage is getting better and better because God is at the center.

❖ Every day my marriage grows more passionate and enduring relying on God's strength.

❖ Every day my partner and I fall in love again.

❖ I will always keep a sense of humor about small

issues that arise in my marriage.

❖ I will always look for ways that I can contribute to my partner's happiness.

❖ I will always remember our wedding anniversary and find loving ways to celebrate it.

❖ I always treat my partner with infinite respect.

❖ I am a fantastic wife.

❖ I am a loving and faithful wife.

❖ I am a loving and loyal husband.

❖ I am a supportive, loving, spouse.

❖ It is my heart's desire that you always start and end your day in prayer.

Prayer of Restoration

Dear Heavenly Father,

So much of our time is taken up, just keeping up with the demands of life unexpected. Responsibilities can be overwhelming and simply exhausting some days. So many things require and command our attention, our thoughts, and our time. Help us to slow down to hear Your still small voice, Lord. Give us the wisdom, and patience to manage our days, so that we have ample time for each other and more importantly, time for You. Draw us closer together through understanding, forgiveness, compassion, and trust.

Teach us to unwind in each other's presence, and to restore one another with encouraging words, and little kind gestures that say, "you matter." One of the most refreshing things one can have in the hustle and grind of everyday living are the soothing arms of a lover who welcomes us home with a heart for God. Jesus, help us to find that place of refuge and strength in each other. In Jesus' name, we pray. Amen.

"But the wisdom that is from above is first pure, then peaceable, gentle, and easy to be intreated, full of mercy and good fruits, without partiality, and without hypocrisy.

And the fruit of righteousness is sown in peace of them that make peace" (James 3:17-18, KJV).

<u>Notes</u>

About the Author

Shenine is an author and the founder and owner of Purposely Blessed, LLC, a Christian Ministry and faith-based business whose mission is to spread the Word of God through custom apparel and merchandise she personally designs and crafts. Shenine is an Army veteran and holds a BA in Healthcare Administration. She resides in Columbia, SC with her husband, teenaged son, and three daughters. Their oldest son is currently serving in the Army as well. Shenine publishes a Christian newsletter, devotionals, and other inspirational writings on her website, PurposelyBlessed.com, using her platform to connect with and encourage other women in the United States and from around the world. She is an ambassador and sponsor for Save the Children's efforts in Trinidad and Tobago.